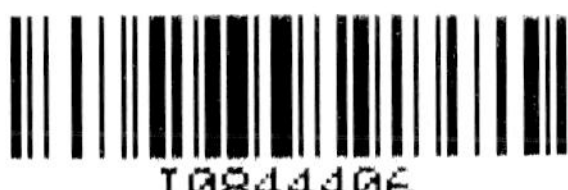

DRAGONS COLORING

book for children

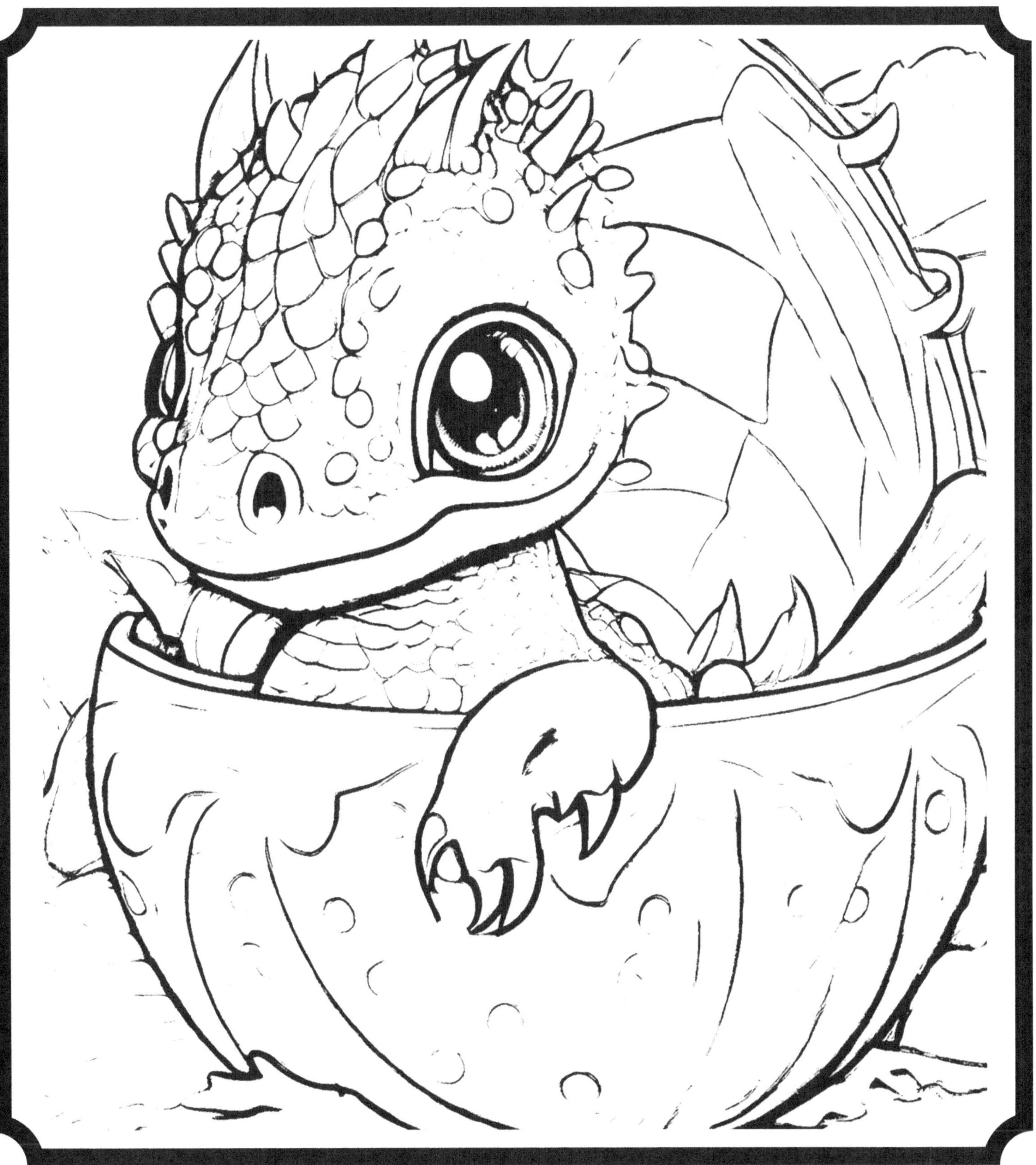

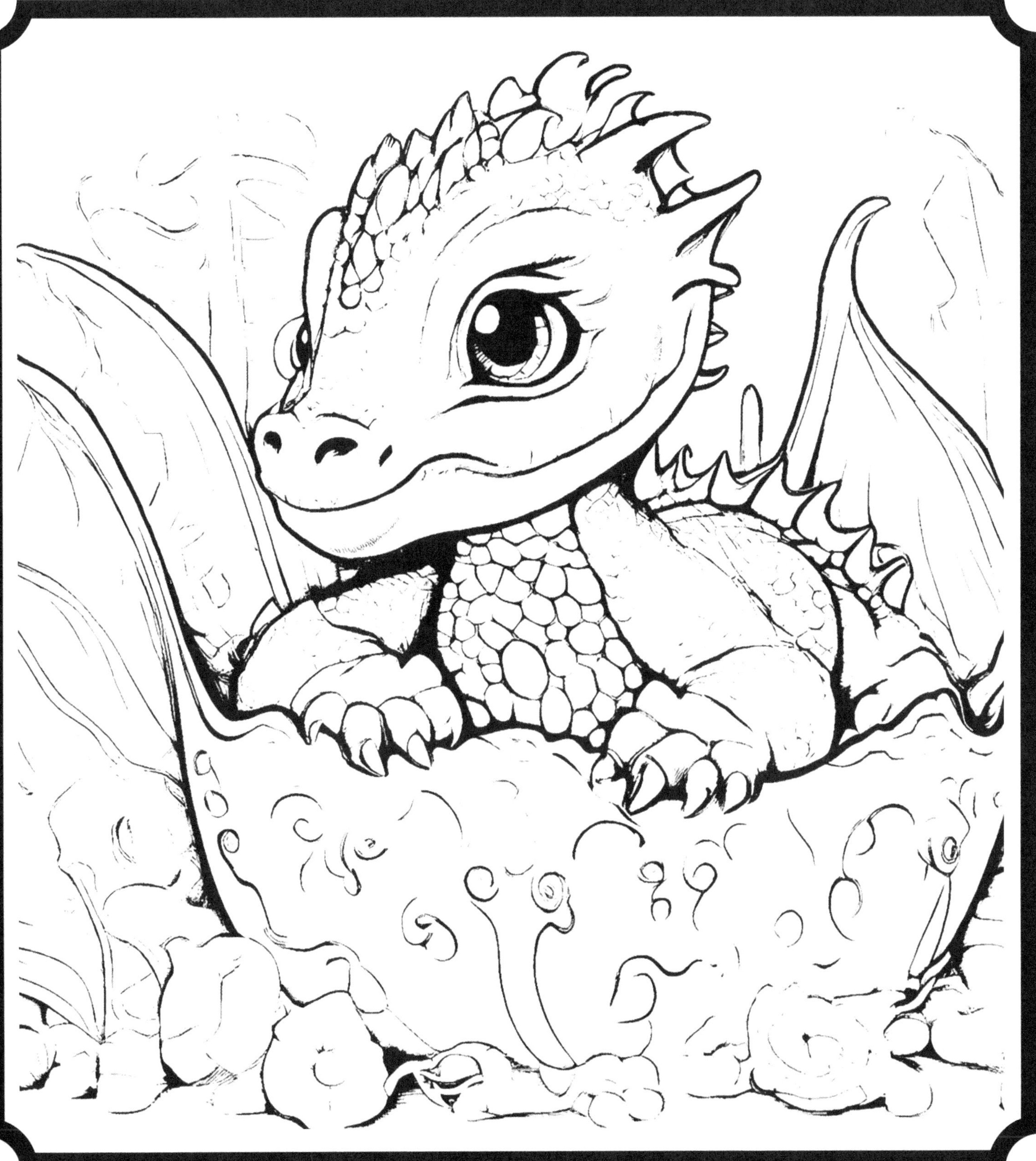

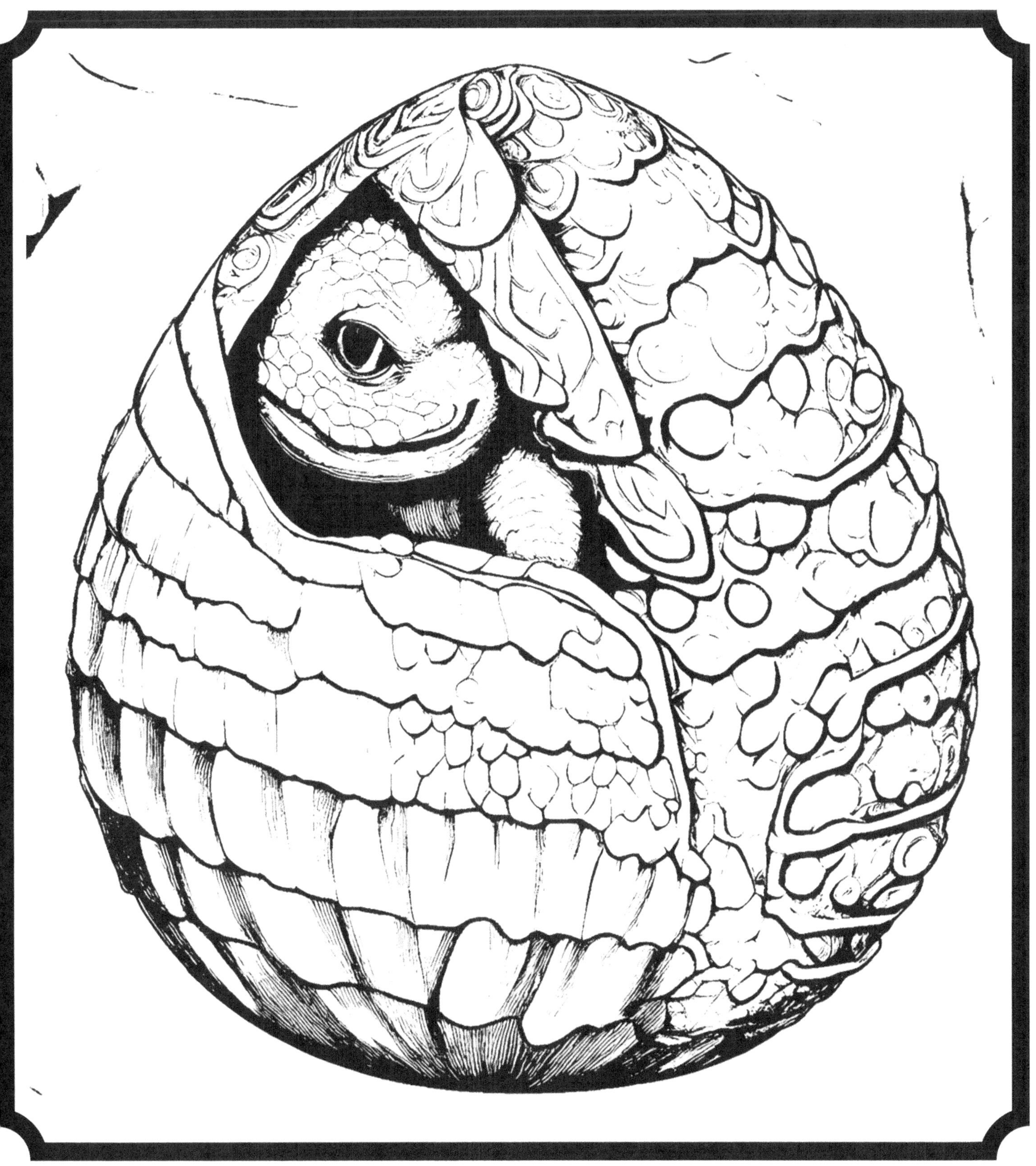

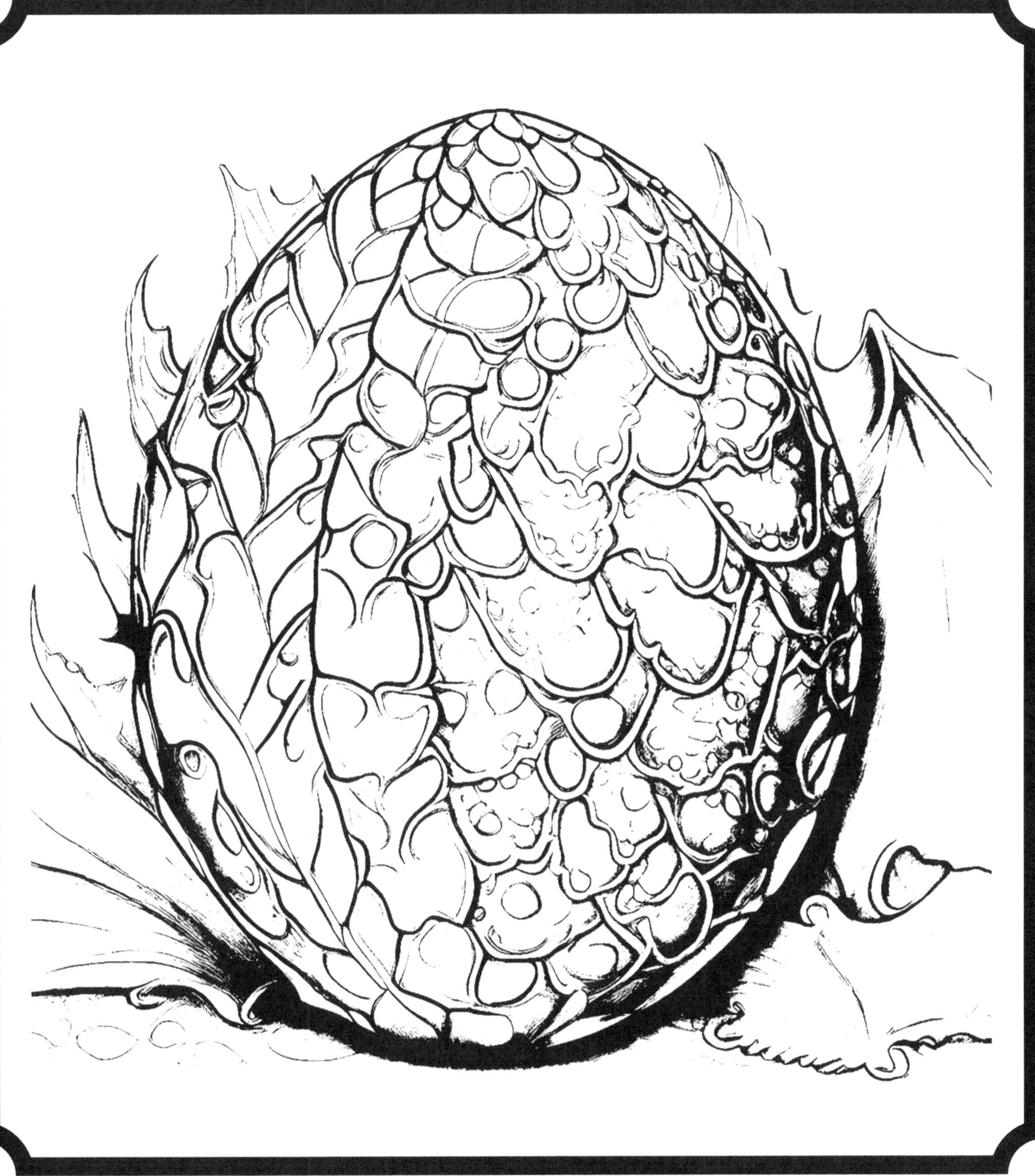

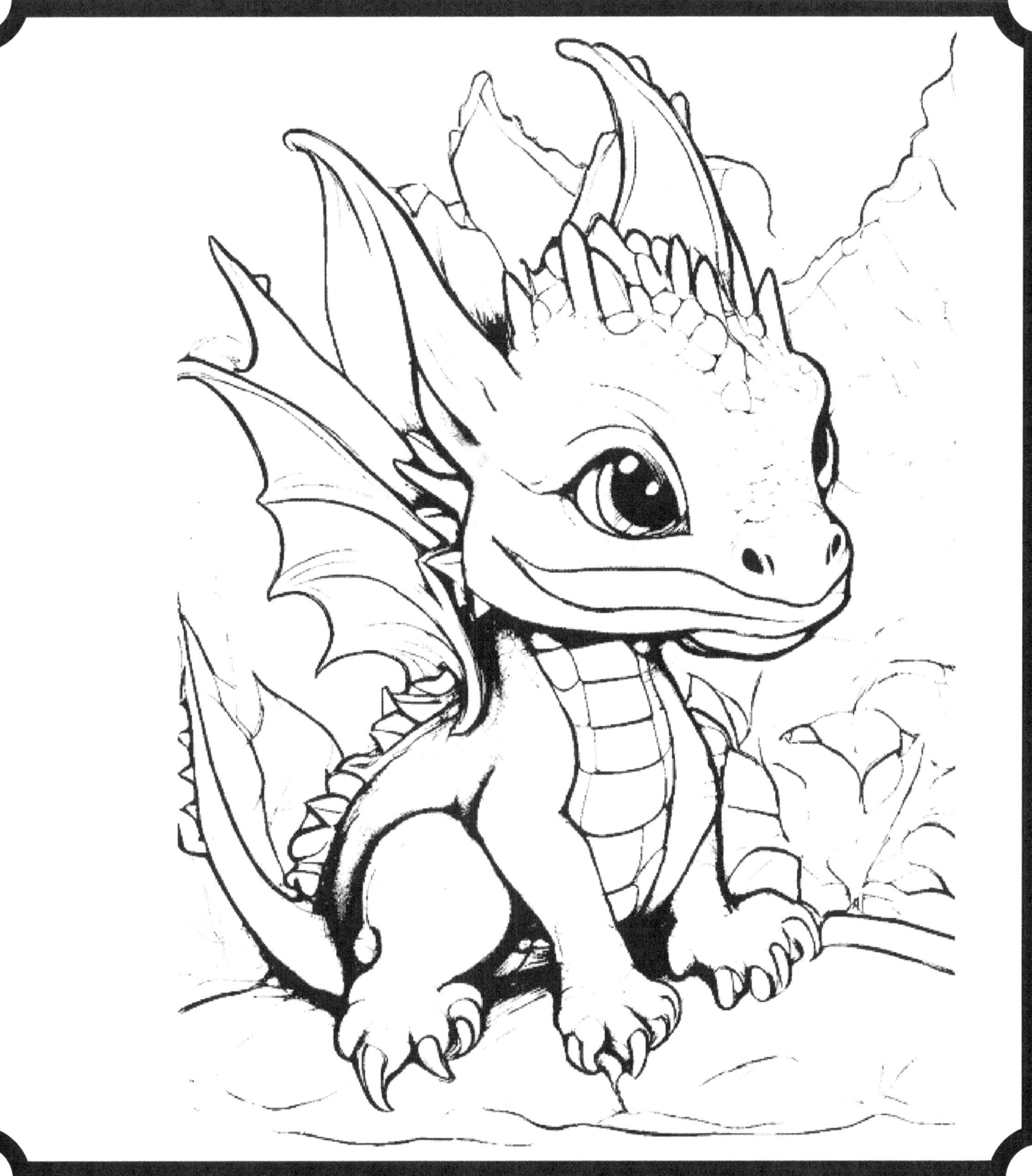

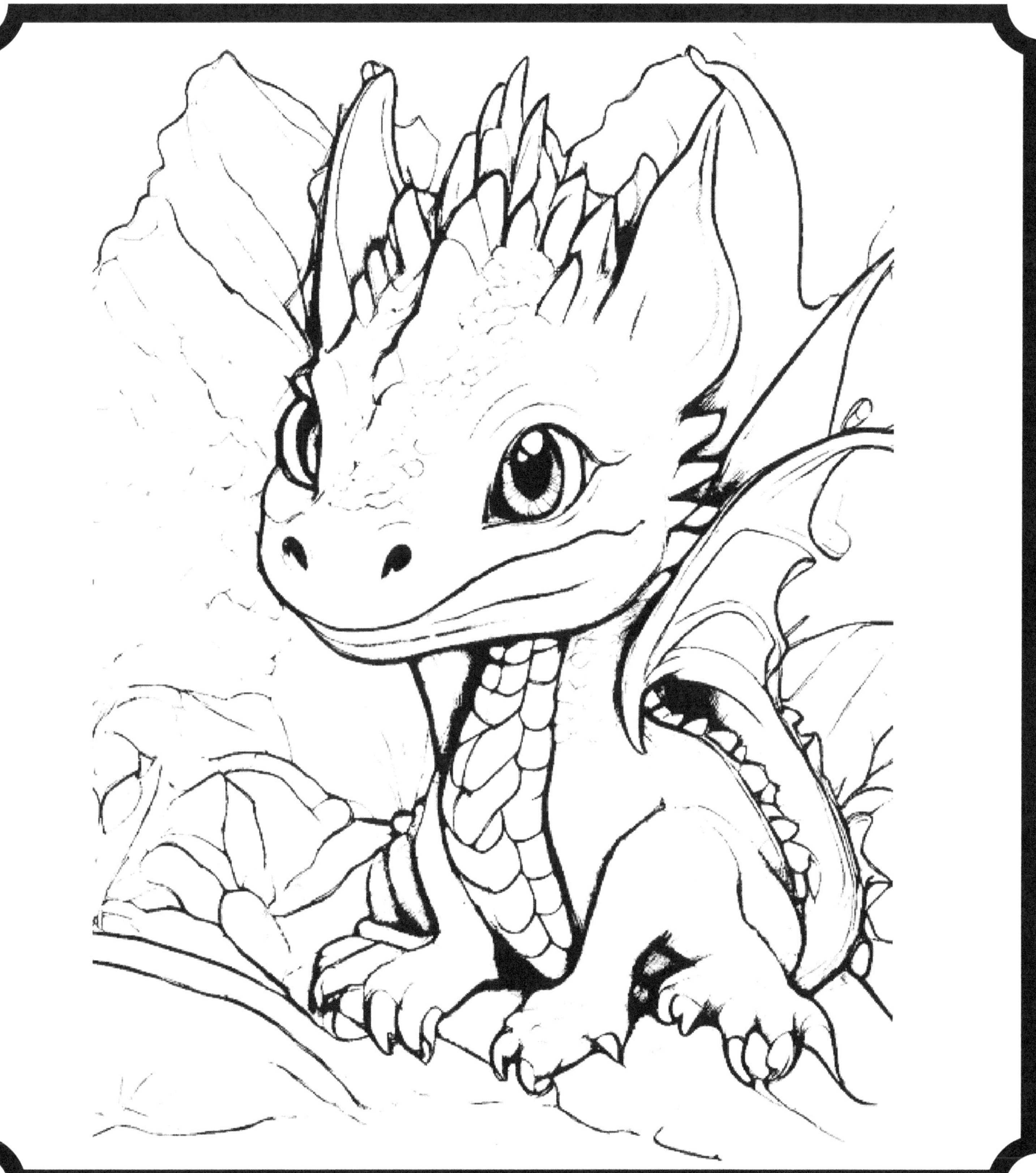

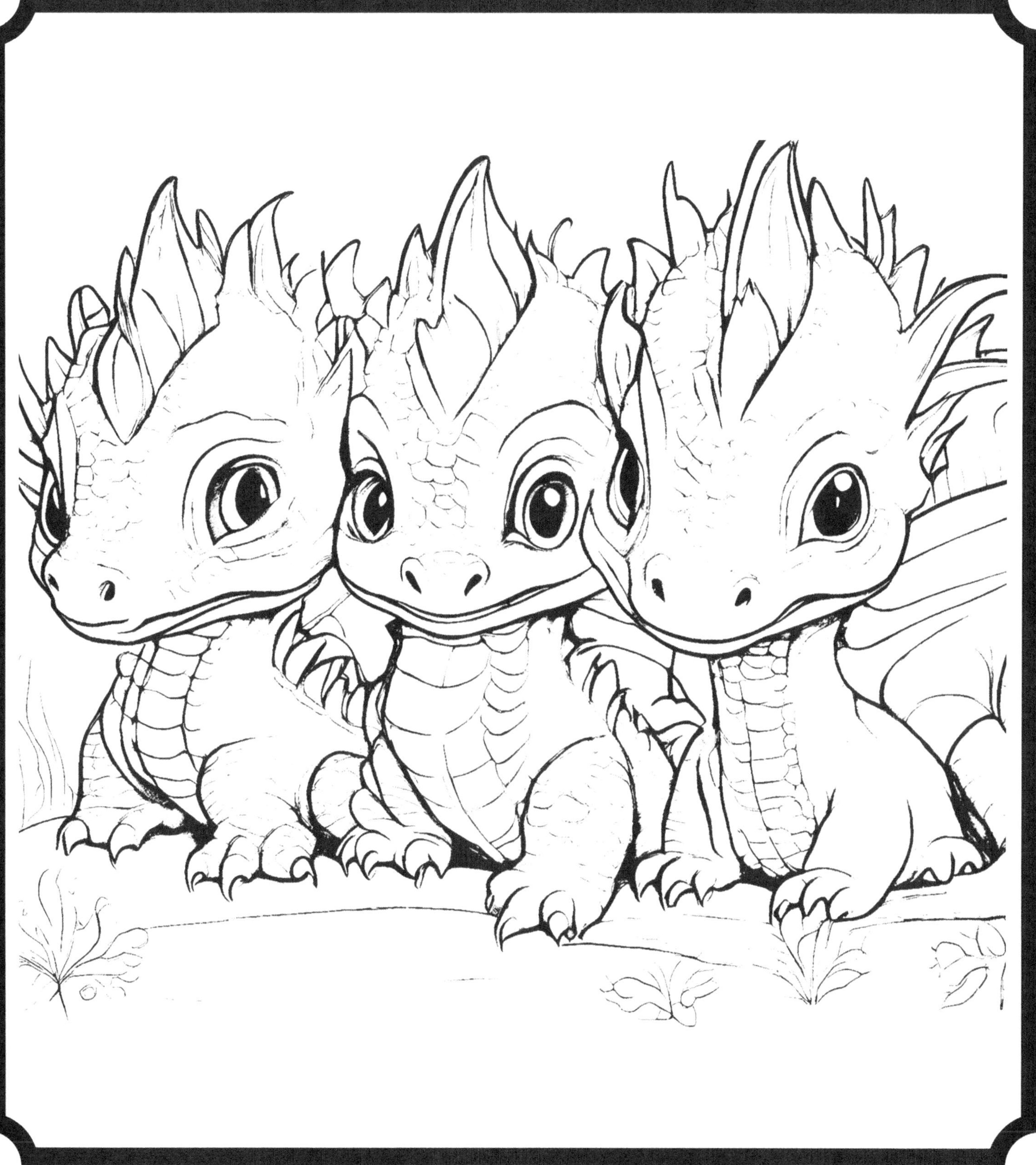

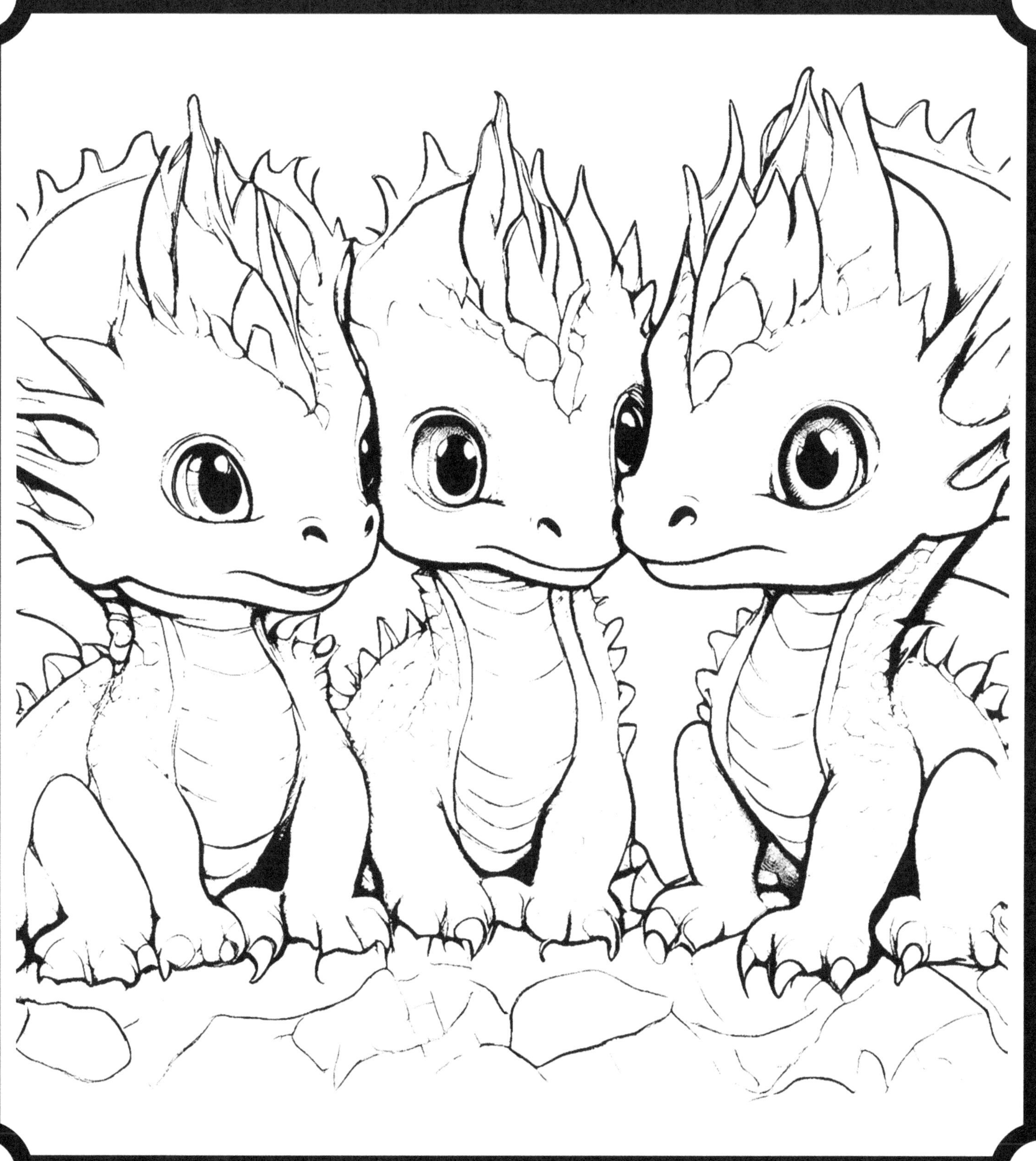

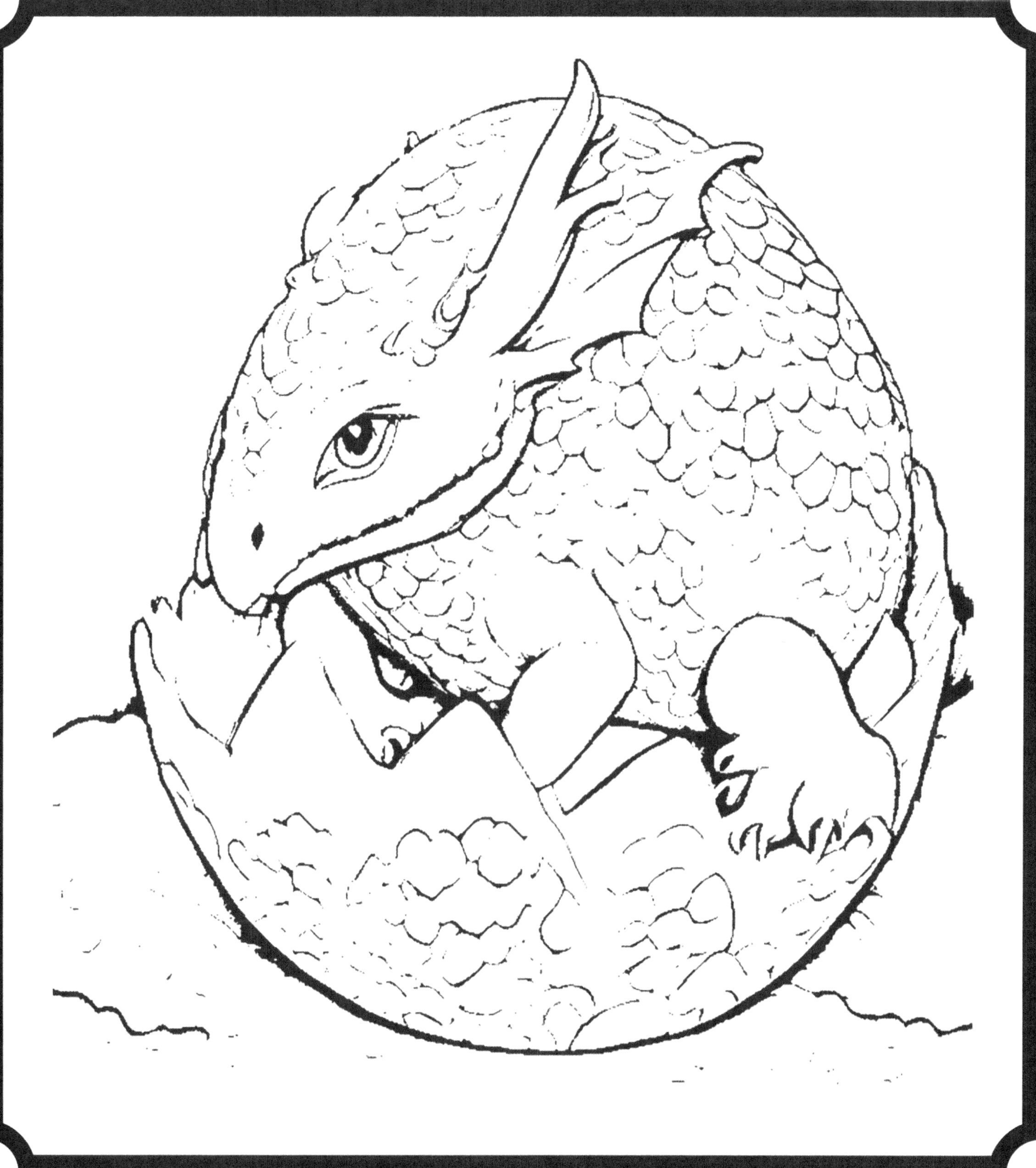

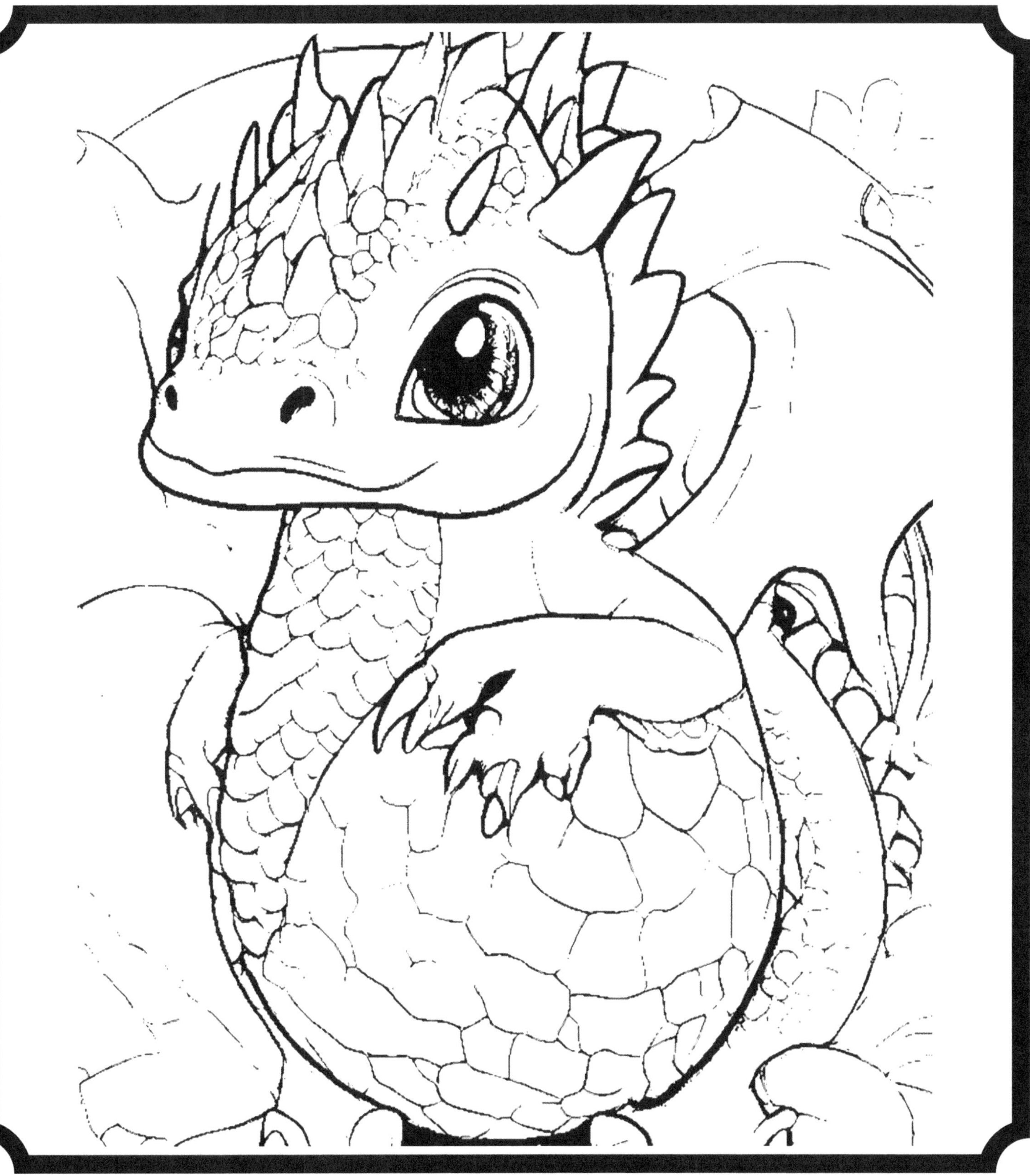

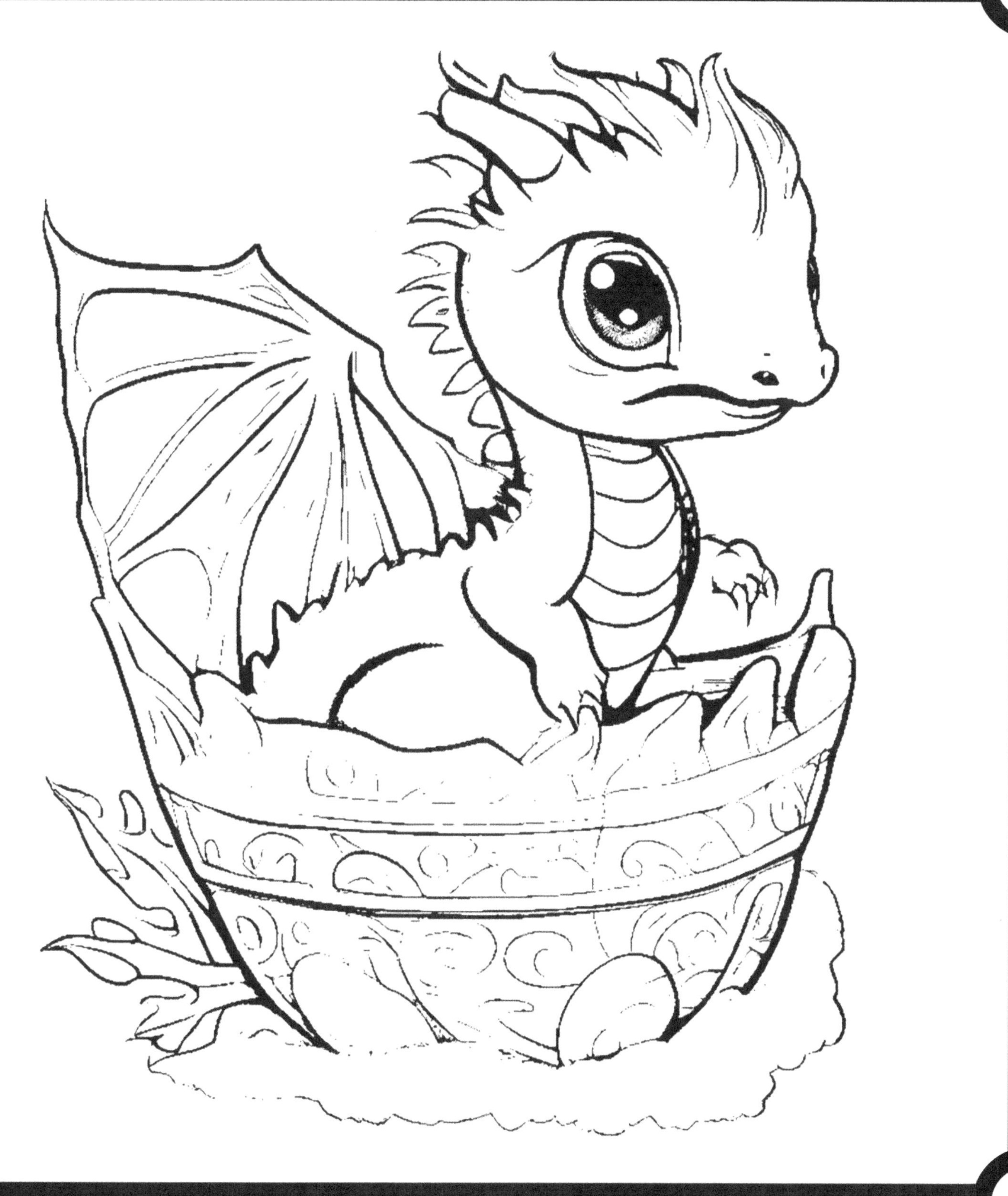

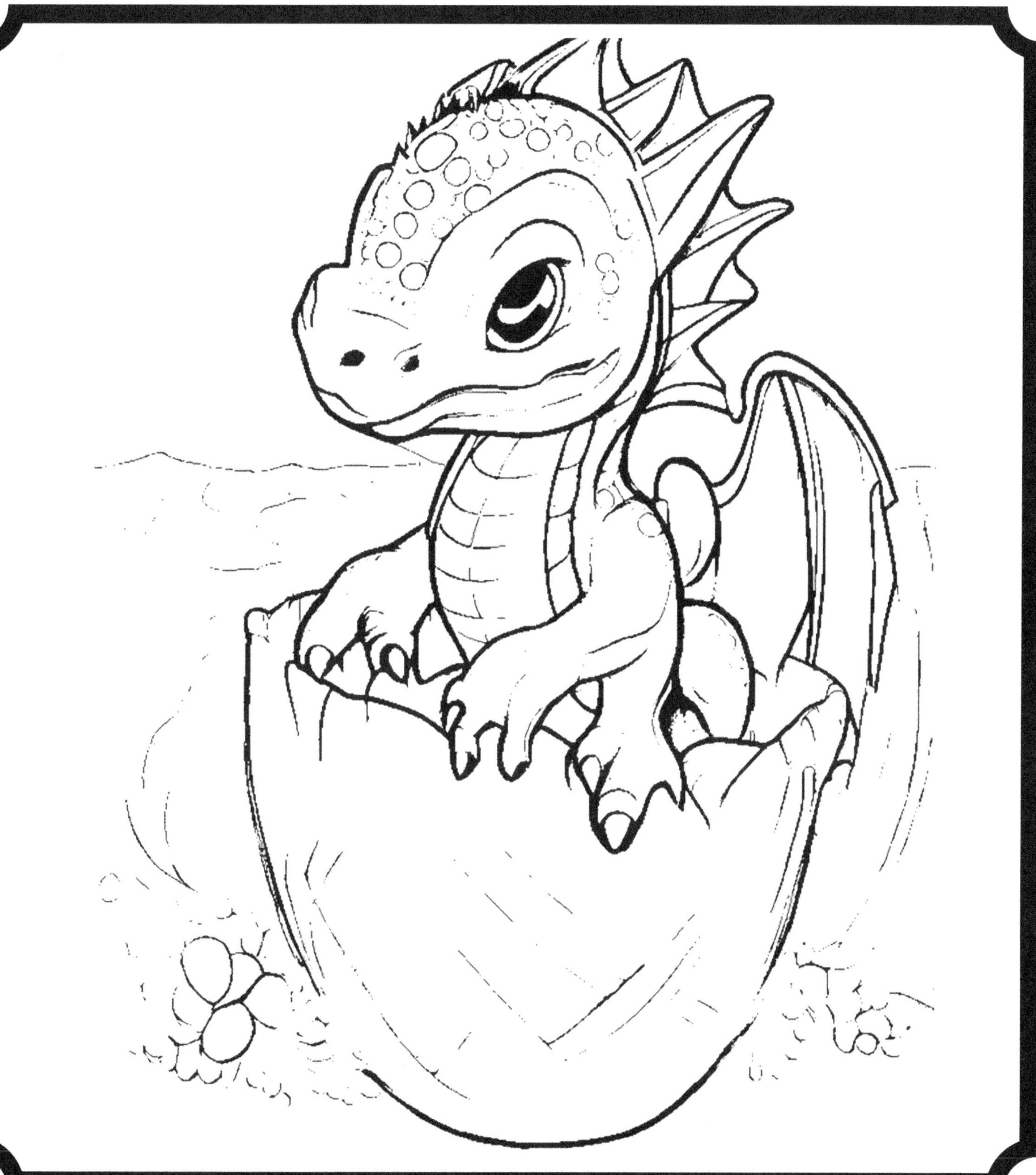

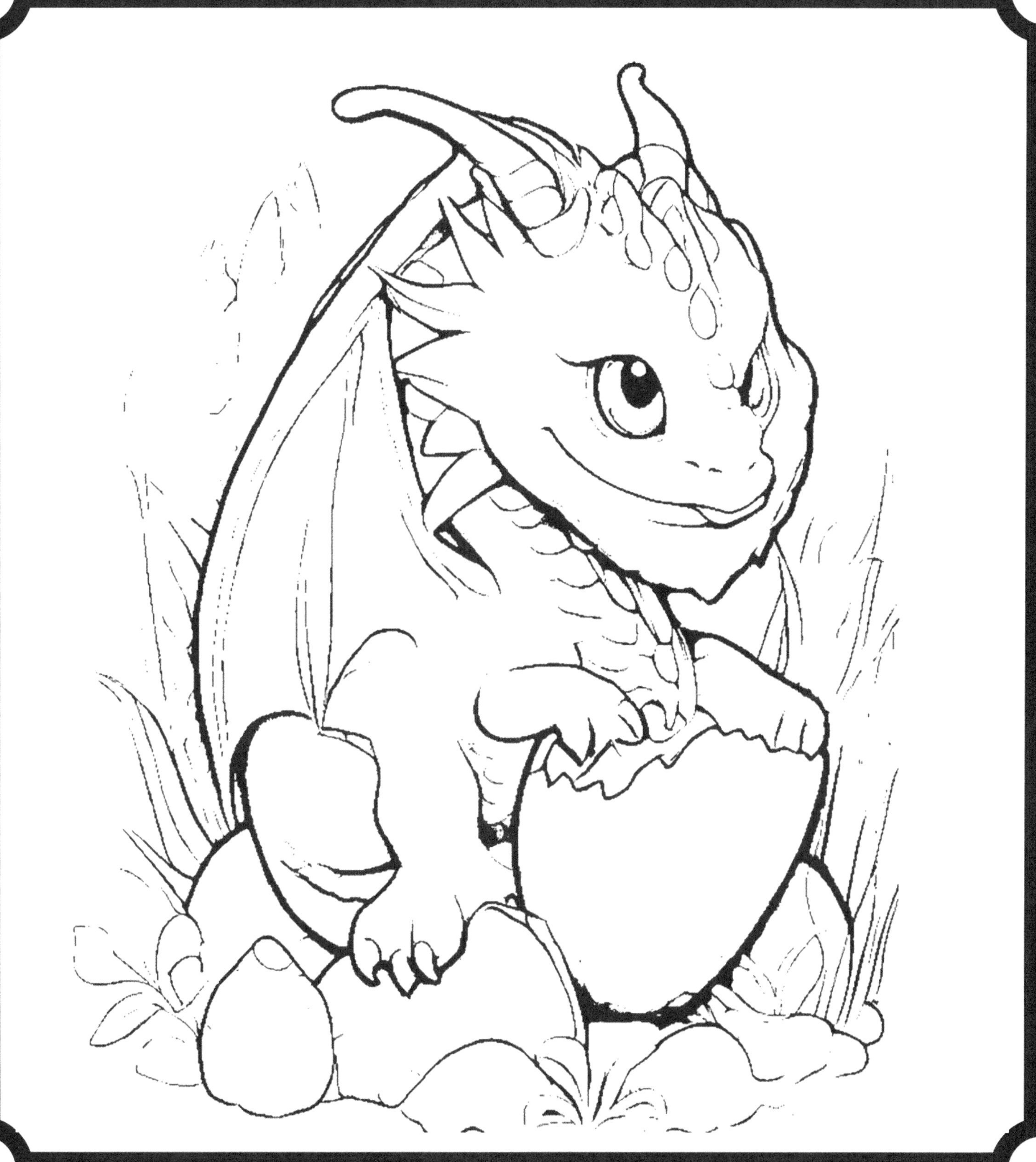

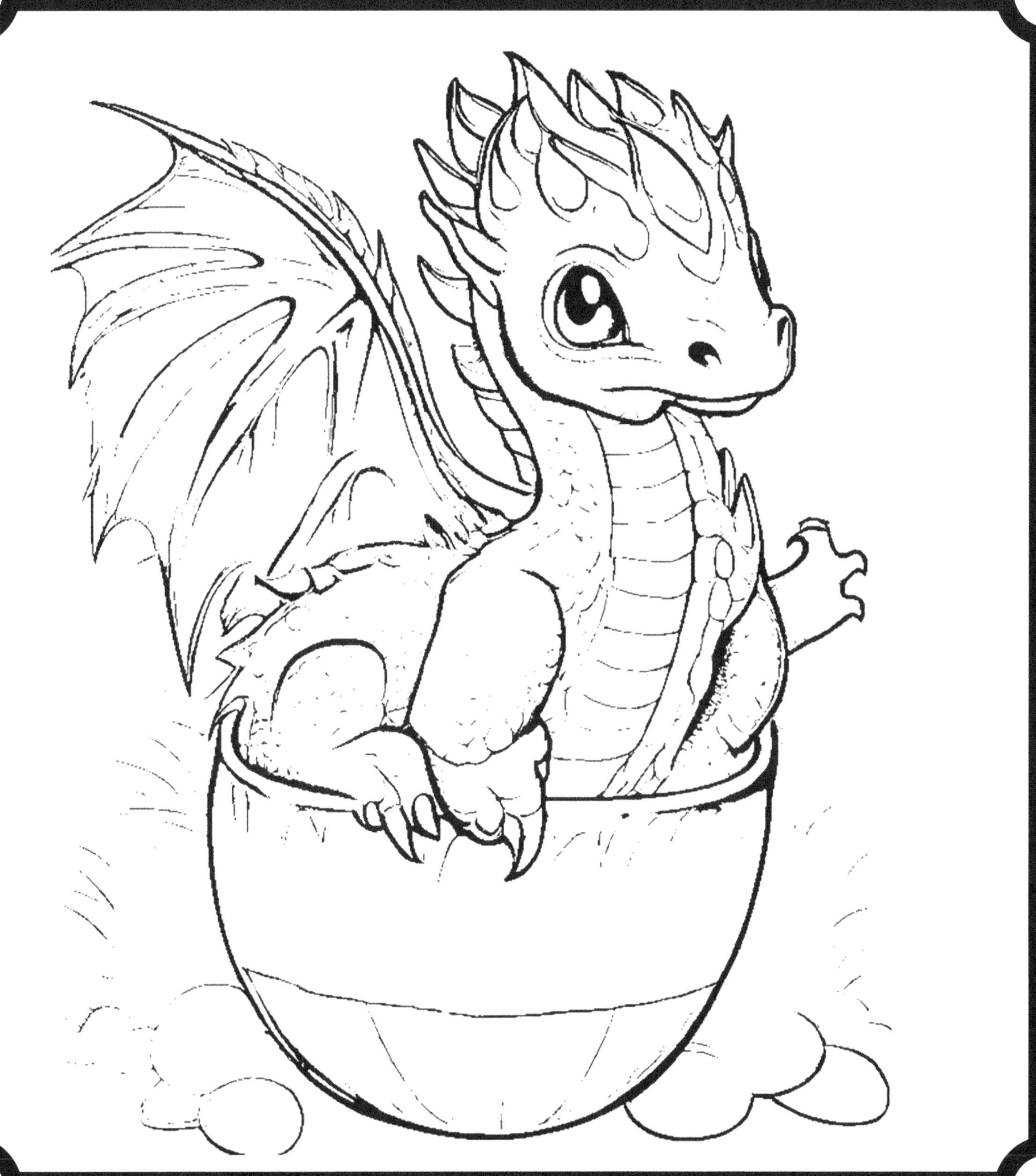

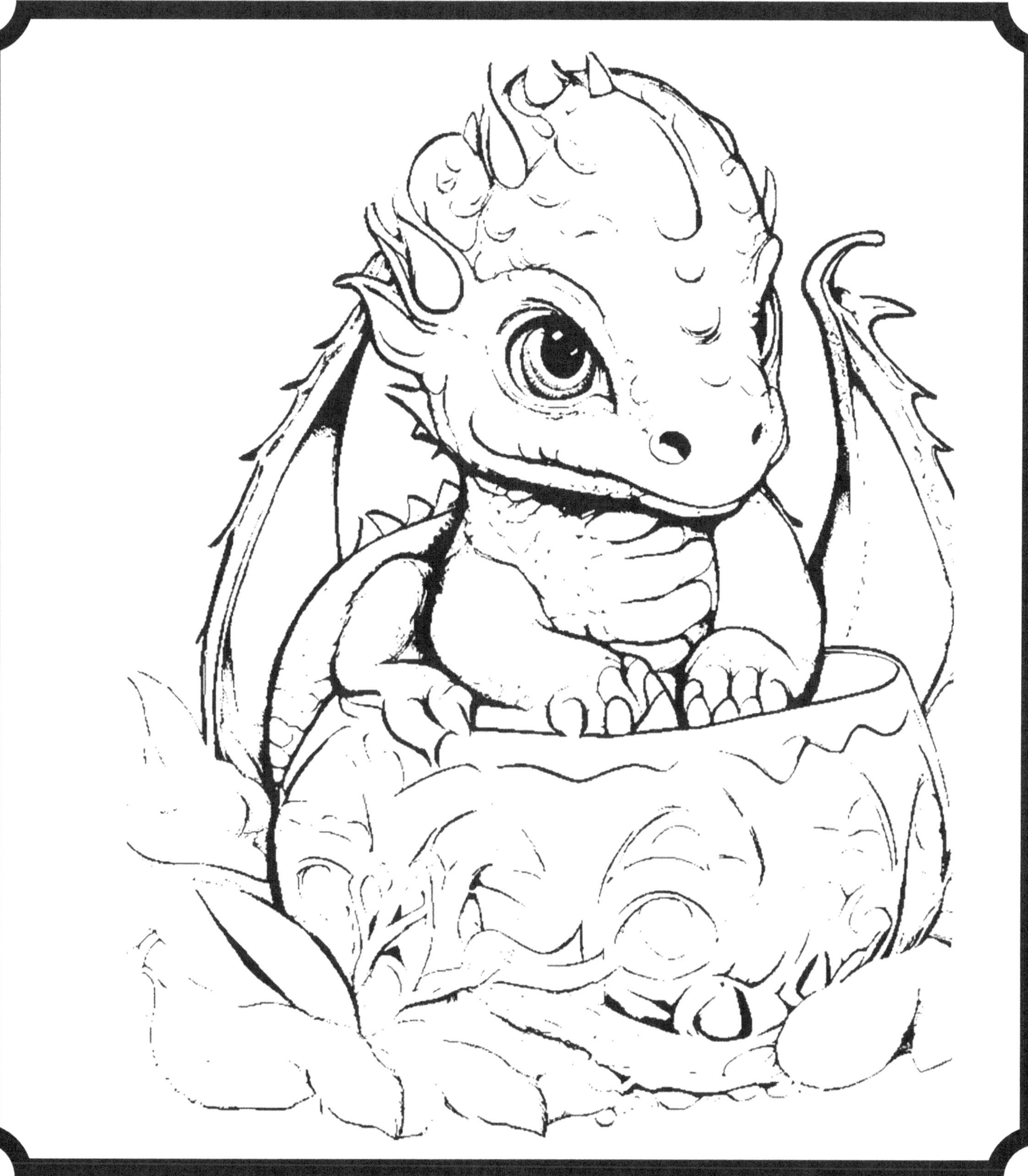